World in Focus
China

ALI BROWNLIE BOJANG AND NICOLA BARBER

WAYLAND

First published in 2006 by Hodder Wayland,
an imprint of Hodder Children's Books

© Wayland 2006

This paperback edition published in 2009 by Wayland,
an imprint of Hachette Children's Books,
338 Euston Road, London NW1 3BH
www.hachettelivre.co.uk

Commissioning editor: Victoria Brooker
Editor: Nicola Barber
Inside design: Chris Halls, www.mindseyedesign.co.uk
Cover design: Wayland

Series concept and project management by EASI-Educational Resourcing
(info@easi-er.co.uk)
Statistical research: Anna Bowden
Maps and graphs: Martin Darlison, Encompass Graphics

British Library Cataloguing in Publication Data
Brownlie, Alison, 1949-
    China. - (World in focus)
    1. China - Juvenile literature
    I. Title II. Barber, Nicola
    951'.06

ISBN 978 0 7502 4702 3

Printed and bound in China

Cover top: A teenage girl wearing traditional costume in Wengxiang, southeast China.
Cover bottom: Great Wall, north of Beijing.
Title page: Great Wall, Simatai.

Picture acknowledgements. The author and publisher would like to thank the
following for allowing their pictures to be reproduced in this publication:
Corbis 9 (top) (Burstein Collection), 9 (bottom), 14 and 54 (Keren Su), 11 and 13 (Bettmann), 15, 16, 17, 23, 24
and 26 (Reuters), 18 (Kin Cheung/Reuters), 21 (Andrew Holbrooke), 22 (Guang Nin/Reuters), 27 and 40
(China Photos/Reuters), 29 (China Span, LLC), 30 and 31 (Claro Cortes IV/Reuters), 36 (Corbis), 45 (top)
(Bohemian Nomad Picturemakers), 45 (bottom) (China Newsphoto/Reuters), 46 (Liu Liquu) 49 (Jason
Lee/Reuters), 51 (Issei Kato/Reuters), 55 (Craig Lovell), 58 (Yang Liu), 59 (Wang Jianmin/Xinhua Photos);
EASI-Images cover top, title page 12, 19, 28, 33, 34, 38, 39, 41, 53 and 56 (Adrian Cooper), 4, 32, 47 and 48
(Tony Binns), 37 (Roy Maconachie); Chris Fairclough cover bottom, 5, 8, 10, 20, 25, 42, 43, 50 and 52; Ed
Parker 57.

The website addresses (URLs) included in this book were valid at the time of going to press.
However, because of the nature of the Internet, it is possible that some addresses may have
changed, or sites may have changed or closed down since publication. While the author and
Publishers regret any inconvenience this may cause the readers, no responsibility for any such
changes can be accepted by either the author or the Publisher.

The directional arrow portrayed on the map on page 7 provides only an approximation of north.
The data used to produce the graphics and data panels in this title were the latest available at the
time of production.

CONTENTS

CHAPTER 1

China – An Overview

China covers a vast area of eastern Asia and is home to one-fifth of the world's total population. Its culture and history stretch back over four thousand years, making it one of the oldest civilizations in the world. The Chinese once believed that their country was at the centre of the geographical world, and they named it *Zhongguo* – 'Middle Earth' or 'Middle Country'. The name China probably comes from one of the early dynasties that ruled the country, the Qin (Ch'in).

▼ These spectacular limestone hills are found in the valley of the Li River, near Guilin, in Guangxi Province, south China. Fields of rice cover the floor of the valley.

▲ East and West meet in Nanjing Road, Shanghai, a wide shopping street where consumers can buy anything from live scorpions to Ford cars. People can also buy food 24 hours a day from traditional street vendors or Western fast-food outlets.

RAPID CHANGE

Today, nowhere in the world is changing as fast, and on such a scale, as China. However, for thousands of years China changed very little. It was ruled by a series of dynasties (in which power is handed down within the same family), and the vast majority of the population worked on the land. In the early 20th century China threw off its dynastic rule and in 1949 it became a Communist state. Towards the end of the century, China's government introduced huge reforms which led to it becoming one of the major world economies – some international organizations now predict that China will overtake the United States and Europe to become the world's largest economy by 2025.

While the vast majority of Chinese people have yet to benefit from China's economic boom, and millions still live in poverty, for a few the changes have meant more affluence and an increasingly Western lifestyle. The factors that led to the success of China's economic growth – abundant natural resources, a large workforce, good infrastructure and a stable society – have long been there, but in the past China was reluctant to develop relationships with other countries. Today, however, China's wealth is based on manufacturing and exporting products to the rest of the world. This change has involved a major shift in the thinking of the Communist party that still governs China.

BIG POPULATION, BIG COUNTRY

China is the most populous nation on earth: in 2005 its population was estimated to be 1.33 billion. The size of its population is one of China's strengths, giving it a large workforce and a massive internal consumer market, but at the same time the Chinese government is faced with the challenge of feeding and ensuring the welfare of this vast populace.

Geographically, China is the third largest country in the world after Russia and Canada, with a huge range of different landscapes and climates. In the past its vast size hindered its development, but today many new railways and roads are being built and there has been a massive increase in air traffic within the country to move people and goods around

quickly and efficiently. These changes, and many others, make China a country that is a fascinating mix of the ancient and the ultra-modern; of the traditional and the high-tech.

Physical geography

- Land area: 9,326,410 sq km/ 3,600,927 sq miles
- Water area: 270,550 sq km/ 104,459 sq miles
- Total area: 9,596,960 sq km/ 3,705,386 sq miles
- World rank (by area): 3
- Land boundaries: 22,147 km/ 13,753 miles
- Border countries: Afghanistan, Bhutan, Burma, India, Kazakhstan, North Korea, Kyrgystan, Laos, Mongolia, Nepal, Pakistan, Russia, Tajikistan, Vietnam
- Coastline: 14,500 km/ 9,005 miles
- Highest point: Mount Everest (8,850 m/ 29,035 ft)
- Lowest point: Turpan Pendi (-154 m/ -505 ft)

Source: CIA World Factbook

▶ The red colour of the Chinese flag symbolizes revolution. The large star represents the Communist party while the four smaller stars signify the Chinese people. The flag was adopted in 1949.

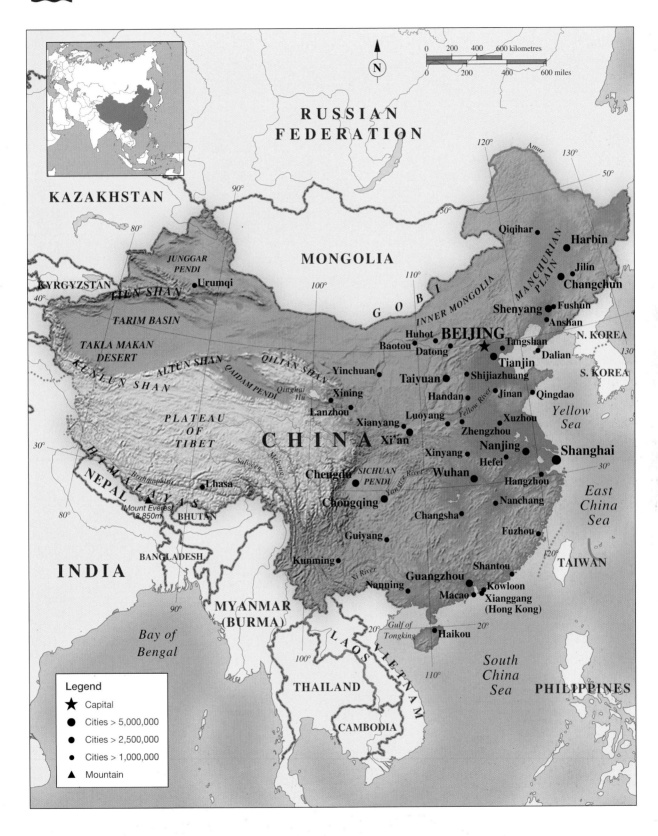

KAZAKHSTAN

RUSSIAN
FEDERATION

N

0   200   400   600 kilometres

0   200   400   600 miles

MONGOLIA

KYRGYZSTAN

*JUNGGAR
PENDI*

● Urumqi

LIEN SHAN

TARIM BASIN

*TAKLA MAKAN
DESERT*

KUNLUN SHAN

ALTUN SHAN

QILIAN SHAN

QAIDAM PENDI

*Qinghai
Hu*

GOBI

INNER MONGOLIA

Huhot ●

Baotou ● Datong ●

● Yinchuan

Xining ●

Lanzhou ●

Qiqihar ●

Harbin

*MANCHURIAN
PLAIN*

Jilin

Changchun

Shenyang ● Fushun ●
● Anshan

N. KOREA

BEIJING ★ Tangshan ●

Tianjin ● Dalian ●

Taiyuan ● ● Shijiazhuang

S. KOREA

Handan ● Jinan ● Qingdao

Yellow River

Luoyang ● Xuzhou ●

*Yellow
Sea*

*PLATEAU
OF
TIBET*

HIMALAYAS

NEPAL

Brahmaputra

Mount Everest
8,850m ▲

BHUTAN

BANGLADESH

INDIA

CHINA

Xianyang ●
Xi'an ●

Zhengzhou ●

Xinyang ●

Nanjing ●

Shanghai

Hefei ●

● Chengdu

*SICHUAN
PENDI*

Wuhan ●

Hangzhou ●

Chongqing ●

Yangtze River

Changsha ●

Nanchang ●

*East
China
Sea*

30°

Lhasa ●

Salween

Mekong

Guiyang ●

Fuzhou ●

MYANMAR
(BURMA)

*Bay of
Bengal*

Kunming ●

Xi River

Nanning ●

Guangzhou ●

Shantou ●

Macao ●

Kowloon ●

Xianggang
(Hong Kong)

TAIWAN

*Gulf of
Tongking*

● Haikou

*South
China
Sea*

PHILIPPINES

THAILAND

LAOS

VIETNAM

CAMBODIA

Legend
★ Capital
● Cities > 5,000,000
● Cities > 2,500,000
● Cities > 1,000,000
▲ Mountain

Amur

120°   130°

50°

50°

90°   100°   110°

80°

40°

30°

80°

90°   100°   110°   120°   130°

30°

20°   20°

CHAPTER 2

History

For most of the country's history, dynasties of emperors ruled China. One of the earliest dynasties, the Chou (Zhou) dynasty (c.1046-221 BC), introduced the first feudal system – well over a thousand years before it existed in Europe. Under the feudal system, supporters of the emperor were given domains, areas of land, in return for their loyalty and for military and other services. The land of these domains was worked by peasants who produced food and wealth for their lords, and received protection in return.

ANCIENT CHINA

Over the centuries, China's borders expanded and contracted following conquests and incursions. Most dynasties were eventually brought down by revolutions or rebellions, or by invasions. The times between dynasties were often periods of chaos when various warlords vied for power. The threat of invasion from Central Asia led to the construction of the Great Wall of China. The wall was built during the Qin dynasty, from about 214 BC, to prevent incursions by Mongol tribes. It was extended westwards during the Han dynasty, and over the centuries was rebuilt and extended several times more.

◀ Tourists from all over the world, including many from China itself, flock to see the Great Wall north of Beijing. The wall extends about 6,400 km (4,000 miles) across northern China.

CHINESE DYNASTIES

Date	Dynasty
c.2070-c.1600 BC	**Xia** Some of the world's first towns built.
c.1600-c.1046 BC	**Shang** Writing system developed.
c.1046-c.221 BC	**Chou (Zhou)** Feudal system established.
221-206 BC	**Qin** First unification of China as a centralized state. Military expeditions push forward the frontiers in the north and south. Construction of the Great Wall begins, to deter invaders from Central Asia.
206 BC-AD 220	**Han** Flourishing of intellectual, literary and artistic life. Paper and porcelain invented. Improved methods for planting crops. Westward expansion. Trade with Central Asia starts along the 'Silk Road'.
AD 220-280	**Wei, Shu** and **Wu** Period of chaos and decline: China divided into three kingdoms. Growth of Taoism and Buddhism.
AD 265-589	**Jin, Sixteen Kingdoms** and **Northern** and **Southern Dynasties.**
581-618	**Sui** Reunification and centralization of government.
618-907	**T'ang** High point in Chinese civilization: 'golden age' of literature and art.
907-60	**Five Dynasties** Several dynasties struggle for power. China experiences military invasions and breaks up into separate states.
960-1279	**Song** Reunification of China. Development of cities as centres of trade and industry.
1215	Mongols, led by Genghis Khan, capture Beijing.
1279-1368	**Yuan** Kublai Khan (grandson of Genghis Khan) captures the rest of China and establishes Yuan dynasty. Mongols begin to lose their power in the 14th century.
1368-1644	**Ming** Mongols driven out of Beijing. Population doubles and economy booms.
1644-1911	**Ch'ing** or **Manchu** Expansion of territory. In the late 19th century, foreign governments gain control over parts of China.

◀ This bronze vessel dates back to the early Shang dynasty.

Focus on: Confucius

The philosophies of Confucius (K'ung Fu-tzu; c.551-c.479 BC) have had a great influence on the Chinese national character. Confucius emphasized the importance of the social order and from this developed an elaborate set of rules by which he thought people ought to live. He taught his ideas to over 3,000 disciples who recorded his teachings in a book called the *Analects*. Confucius' ideas about the importance of learning, and family and social ties were used as the basis of law from the Han dynasty (206 BC-AD 220) onwards. His ideas also spread to other countries such as Japan, Korea and Vietnam.

▶ This bronze statue of Confucius stands outside the Confucius Temple in Nanjing, eastern China.

CHINA AND EUROPE

For centuries, China outpaced the rest of the world in the arts and sciences. During the T'ang dynasty (618-907), the capital city, Ch'ang-an (today known as Xi'an), was the largest city anywhere in the world, with a population of over one million people (London and Paris did not reach this size for another 1,000 years). Chinese inventions such as the compass, the abacus, fireworks and gunpowder impressed Western visitors to China. One of the first Europeans to go to China was a Venetian traveller, Marco Polo. Marco Polo left Venice in 1271 and spent more than fifteen years in China before returning home in 1295 with stories of the country's efficient postal system, the use of coal as a fuel and a canal-based transport system.

European interest in trading with China started as early as the 16th century, but the Chinese emperors had little desire for the goods offered

▼ The Hall of Supreme Harmony in the Imperial Palace, Beijing, was built in the 15th century. It was used for grand, ceremonial occasions.

by the European traders. The emperors were suspicious of foreigners, fearing that they would attempt to gain power in China, and of the Christian missionaries who tried to establish their faith in China. In 1760, the Chinese government restricted European merchants to the southern port of Guangzhou.

THE OPIUM WARS

By the beginning of the 19th century, China was exporting huge amounts of products such as tea and silk to Europe. But while many European countries and the United States were increasingly interested in opportunities for trade with China, the Chinese emperor stated that China had 'no need' for foreign products. However, there was one import that was becoming increasingly popular in China – opium. The opium trade was seen by the British government as one solution to its trade imbalance with China, and during the 18th century British merchants imported increasing quantities of the drug. The increased availability

◀ The British navy bombards Guangzhou in 1841, during the First Opium War.

of opium had a devastating effect on Chinese society as thousands of people became addicts, and in 1800 the Chinese banned its import. The First Opium War (1839–42) was fought after the Chinese seized illegal stocks of opium in Guangzhou. The Chinese were defeated and, under the Treaty of Nanjing, China opened several ports to foreign trade and ceded the island of Hong Kong to the British. After further defeat in the Second Opium War (1856-60) and a disastrous war against Japan (1894-5), China was forced to cede more territory and to allow more foreign access to its ports and trade.

THE END OF THE DYNASTIES

By the beginning of the 20th century, foreign demands and internal rebellions had completely eroded the power of the Ch'ing dynasty. In 1911, revolutionary forces led by Sun Yat-Sen finally deposed the last Ch'ing emperor, ending 3,000 years of dynastic rule in China. China was proclaimed a republic in 1912. The revolutionary forces joined together to create the Nationalist Party (Kuomintang), but almost immediately the country fragmented, with rival warlords fighting for power. At the end of World War I, under the terms of the Treaty of Versailles, China once again lost territory as Japan was allowed to take over former German territories in China. On 4 May 1919, a group of students demonstrated in Tiananmen Square in Beijing against the treaty. This demonstration was part of a wave of nationalism that became known as the Fourth of May movement, and which led to the formation of the Chinese Communist Party in 1921. During the 1920s, the Communists joined with the Nationalists (led by Chiang Kai-shek after the death of Sun Yat-Sen in 1925) to try to reunify China.

Focus on: The Boxer uprising

The 'Boxers' was a secret society whose members wanted to throw all the 'foreign devils' (foreigners) out of China. In 1900, thousands of young people attacked symbols of European power and influence, such as embassies and Christian missions. They marched on Beijing, attracting more followers on the way, and laid siege to areas of the city for two months. Eventually an international force of European and American soldiers put down the rebellion.

▲ This huge portrait of Mao Zedong hangs at Tiananmen Gate, the main entrance to the Imperial Palace in Beijing.

NATIONALISTS AND COMMUNISTS

The alliance between the Kuomintang and the Communists soon became strained. In 1927 Chiang Kai-shek's Nationalists attacked the Communists and forced many Communist leaders to go into hiding. The Kuomintang established a government with its capital at Nanjing, and from 1931 fought a civil war against the Communists. However, in the same year Japan began to threaten China, occupying Manchuria and advancing across northern China. Full-scale war between Japan and China broke out in 1937. Both the Nationalists and the Communists fought a guerrilla campaign against the Japanese invaders, but after the surrender of Japan in 1945, at the end of World War II, civil war between the two sides resumed.

During the war with Japan, the Communists had become both strong and popular under their leader, Mao Zedong, and it was the Communists who emerged victorious in the years after World War II. By 1949 they had defeated the Kuomintang, forcing Chiang Kai-shek and his supporters to flee to Taiwan, an island off the east coast of China. There, with US support, the Nationalists set up an alternative Chinese government. In Beijing, Mao Zedong proclaimed the creation of the world's second Communist state (after the Soviet Union), the People's Republic of China.

THE GREAT LEAP FORWARD

With help from its ally, the Soviet Union, Communist China made economic progress in the 1950s. Rapid industrialization increased production, and land was redistributed to create

Focus on: The Long March (1934-5)

After the alliance between the Nationalists and the Communists came to an end in 1927 the Kuomintang, better led and equipped, inflicted heavy defeats on the Communists. In 1934, after several years of fighting, some hundred thousand people, making up the main force of the Communist army, left their base in Jiangxi Province and marched west and then north for over 9,600 km (6,000 miles) in a journey known as the 'Long March'. The survivors – only twenty thousand of the original force – joined other Communists in Yan'an a year later. However, the Long March saw Mao Zedong take control of the Communist army and turn it into a force that would, eventually, defeat the Nationalists.

agricultural co-operatives. In 1958, however, Mao Zedong's government introduced a policy which is estimated to have cost the lives of up to thirty million people.

The aim of the 'Great Leap Forward' was to increase food and steel production through the creation of larger collective farms and new steel mills. Mao Zedong believed that the Communist Party could inspire the Chinese people to work ever harder and overcome all obstacles. In reality, the Great Leap Forward was badly planned and incompetently led. By 1961, following a country-wide famine, the government was forced to admit its costly failure. Mao stepped down from power to be replaced by Liu Shaoqi, a modernizer who was more open to liberal approaches.

THE CULTURAL REVOLUTION

Mao Zedong soon became unhappy about what he saw as the 'capitalist tendencies' of Liu Shaoqi and his supporters. Gradually Mao regained influence and in 1966 he launched the Great Proletarian Cultural Revolution which, in the name of education and restoring true Communist principles, attacked intellectuals and those who were introducing 'bourgeois influences' into China. Students and workers denounced reformers and intellectuals in mass meetings. The Red Guards, mostly school and university students, increasingly used violence against anyone unlucky enough to be considered 'bourgeois' or 'elitist'. Millions of people were forced into manual labour (or re-education, as it was called), many thousands were executed, temples and churches were destroyed and schools shut down. In 1968, Mao disbanded the Red Guards and the army restored order, leaving Mao and his supporters, sometimes called the 'Gang of Four', in power.

THE BEGINNINGS OF ECONOMIC REFORM

Mao Zedong died in 1976. Following his death, there was a struggle between those in the Communist party who believed China should open up to the rest of the world and develop economically (the 'reformers'), and those who opposed such measures (the 'conservatives'). The reformers, led by Deng Xiaoping, gained the upper hand and in 1978 a period of economic modernization began. Trade was opened up to the outside world and farmers were allowed to sell their surplus crops on the open market. Relations with Western countries also improved. The US president Richard Nixon had visited China in 1972, establishing the first links which resulted in the restoring of full diplomatic relations between the United States and China in 1979. The current Chinese premier, Wen Jiabao, is seen as one of a long line of reformers who welcomes economic ties with the United States and other Western countries.

▼ Red Guards parade through the streets of Beijing in 1967, during the Cultural Revolution. They are carrying flags and a portrait of Mao Zedong.

CHAPTER 3

Landscape and Climate

China covers an area of 9,596,960 sq km (3,705,386 sq miles), making it slightly larger than the United States, and almost forty times the size of the UK. As might be expected in such a vast country, its landscapes include almost every type of habitat found anywhere on earth – mountains, deserts, forests and plains. Two-thirds of the country is uplands and mountains, much of which is inhospitable. Less than one-third of China's land is fit for cultivation. The Yangtze River serves as a dividing line between the north and the south regions of the country.

▼ Two bactrian camels in the Takla Makan Desert, which lies in Xinjiang Province, in the far northwest of China.

THE NORTH AND WEST

The north and west are dominated by some of the most mountainous areas in the world, with heights averaging 4,500 m (14,764 feet) above sea level. The world's highest mountain range, the Himalayas, lies partly within China. The Himalaya region is remote, barren and unsettled and forms a natural barrier between China and its western neighbours. To the north of the Himalayas lies a vast area of deserts and high pastures, including the Tibetan plateau.

THE SOUTH AND EAST

From the high altitudes of the west, the land descends towards the low-lying river plains in the east. Many rivers flow into this area, fed by

▲ Floodwaters from the Yangtze River inundate houses in Wuhan, the capital of Hubei Province, on 27 August, 2002. The Yangtze floods every year, but the floods are worse in some years than in others.

melting snow and ice from the mountains, and the alluvial soils that they deposit create extremely fertile floodplains. This area has been farmed for centuries and is where the majority of China's population lives today.

CHINA'S RIVERS

The Chang Jiang (Yangtze River) and Huang He (Yellow River) are the most important rivers in China and support millions of people. However, they can bring great destruction when they flood. The Huang He is known as 'China's Sorrow' because of its regular and destructive floods. In the 1930s, an estimated five million people were drowned when the Huang He burst its banks on two separate occasions.

Focus on: The 'roof of the world'

Covering an area of around 2.5 million sq km (965,000 sq miles) – about a quarter of China's land area – the Tibetan plateau dominates western China. About 80 per cent of this highland plateau lies 3,000 m (9,850 feet) above sea level, and about half of it is over 4,500 m (14,764 feet). In the far west of the country, the plateau meets the Himalayas. Fourteen of the world's peaks over 8,000 m (26,250 feet) lie within the Chinese border. The highest peak in the world, Mount Everest, which stands at an altitude of 8,850 m (29,035 feet), is on the border between China and Nepal. It is little wonder that the Tibetan plateau is known as the 'roof of the world'.

CHINA'S CLIMATES

Due to its vast size and its varied topography, China has many different climates, ranging from bitterly cold, subarctic northern winters to warm, subtropical southern summers. Its climate is dominated by the great seasonal wind reversal known as the Asiatic monsoon.

From May to September, warm, moist air is drawn into China from the Indian and Pacific oceans, bringing rain. From October to April cool, dry air blows out from the centre of Asia. The other important factor in China's climate is altitude.

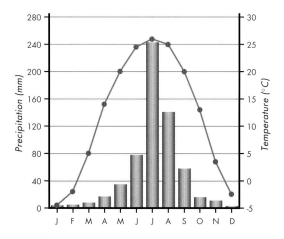

▲ Average monthly climate conditions in Beijing

? Did you know?

Despite its huge size, China uses only one time zone (Greenwich Mean Time (GMT) +8 hours). China covers a longitude range of about 60 degrees, so the country lies across five international time zones (from +5 to +9 hours GMT). This means that in the far northwest, it doesn't get dark until after midnight.

▼ Police patrol the snowclad rooftops of Beijing's Imperial Palace in December 1999. Winters in China's capital city can be bitterly cold.

THE NORTH AND WEST

Temperatures are extreme in the north and west. They are affected by the high altitude and, in winter, by the cold, dry air that blows from Siberia to the north. During the long, severe winters temperatures can sometimes fall as low as -33°C (-27°F) in northern Manchuria – so cold that rivers freeze. Sand dunes covered in snow make a curious sight in the desert areas. By contrast, daytime temperatures in the summer can reach 47°C (117°F) in the desert regions of the northwest, and 38°C (100°F) in Beijing. Dust storms blow up in the deserts in April and May, often carrying sand for thousands of kilometres to cover northern cities such as Beijing. In July and August rainfall is high in Beijing, and the climate becomes humid and uncomfortable. However, to the far north and west, rainfall is more unpredictable, and in some desert areas there is no rainfall at all.

TIBET

Tibet is one of the harshest places on earth. The thin, high-altitude air can neither radiate nor absorb heat, creating extreme temperatures during the day and at night. In the summer, temperatures can reach up to 29°C (84°F) during the day, falling to below 0°C (32°F) at night. During the winters, average minimum temperatures of -10°C (14°F) feel much colder because of the winds, which create wind chill.

THE SOUTH AND EAST

The south and east is partly within the tropics, and in the summer it is the warmest and wettest part of China, as moist air masses from the Pacific Ocean move inland. Summers are generally hot and humid, with average daytime temperatures around 30°C (86°F). Monsoon rainfall is high in the summer, and there is also the possibility of tropical storms, called typhoons, along the southeast coast between July and September. On average there are about five typhoons a year. Winter temperatures average 18°C (64°F), with regular rainfall.

▼ A man walks through the rubble of collapsed buildings after a typhoon hit Shanghai in July 2002. Five people died during the storm.

CHAPTER 4

Population and Settlements

With a huge population of more than 1.3 billion people, China is the most populous nation on earth. China's population has grown rapidly since the founding of the People's Republic, doubling between 1949 and 1987.

ETHNIC GROUPS

There are 56 different ethnic groups in China. The Han Chinese make up 92 per cent of the population, overwhelmingly dominating China. In addition to the Han there are 55 officially recognized ethnic minorities in China. The largest minority group, the Zhuang, mostly live in Guangxi Province, an autonomous region in the south. Chinese Muslims, the Hui, are the second largest ethnic minority, living mainly across the north and central areas of the country. Other minorities include Uyghurs in Xinjiang Province in the northwest, the Tibetans, the Hakka people, and the Mongols who are descended from the nomadic tribes to the north of China.

▼ One of China's minority groups, the Hakka, have a tradition of constructing circular buildings made from earth. These examples are in Xiayang, Fujian Province, eastern China. There are about 30,000 of these structures, which were originally built as a defence against bandits and invaders.

THE ONE-CHILD POLICY

In the 1970s, the Chinese government realized that the country's rapid population growth was harmful to social and economic development, as it became increasingly difficult and costly to ensure employment, housing and medical care for everyone. In 1979, the government began to implement a policy, known as the One-Child Policy, to control population growth. In accordance with this policy, every birth has to be approved by family-planning officials and couples face huge fines if they have more than one child. Second children cannot be registered, so they do not qualify for education or healthcare support.

The restrictions of the One-Child Policy have since been relaxed for some people. Couples from ethnic minorities, parents who are themselves single children, and parents whose first child has been born with physical or mental disabilities may all apply for permission to have second children. Couples in rural areas may also be permitted to have another child if their first baby is a girl.

In terms of controlling population growth the policy has been successful, as birth rates have steadily declined. In 1969, the birth rate was 34.11 per thousand people; by 1998 it had dropped to 16.03 per thousand. The five-year plan for 2006-2010 aims to further decrease China's annual population growth rate. However, the policy has had other, far-reaching effects. It has created a population profile that is rapidly ageing – resulting in fewer people to support elderly parents and grandparents. More controversially, Chinese parents generally prefer to have sons – particularly in rural areas where people tend to

want a child capable of coping with the physical demands of farming. Despite government attempts to encourage people to value girl babies, the practice of aborting female babies, or of abandoning unwanted girls in orphanages, has been widespread since the One-Child Policy was implemented. One result is an imbalance in the Chinese population, with men outnumbering women by almost twelve to one, especially in rural areas. The One-Child Policy has also led to second children being concealed from the authorities, and it is possible that there are tens of millions of unregistered children in China.

▲ This poster in a village in Guizhou Province, southeast China, promotes the Chinese government's One-Child Policy.

 Did you know?

The One-Child Policy has resulted in a generation of single, boy children who are often referred to as China's 'little emperors' because they are so spoilt.

POPULATION DENSITY

Although China's population growth has slowed dramatically, because of its large population-base the number of people in China is still increasing by over 6 million every year. Experts predict that its population may reach nearly 1.5 billion by 2050, although it is likely to be surpassed by India in about 2025 as the world's most populous country.

The population is unevenly spread throughout the country. The average population density in China is 138.6 people per sq km (358.9 per sq mile). But in the densely populated river valleys of the east there are more than 400 people per sq km (1,036 per sq mile), in the central areas 200 people per sq km (518 per sq mile), and in the vast, sparsely populated plateaus of the west there are fewer than 10 people per square km (26 per sq mile).

▼ Construction workers labour on a building project in the city of Xi'an, central China.

URBANIZATION

Most people in China live in rural areas and farm the land. But as the country's economy develops, increasing numbers of people are being attracted to the towns and cities to find work and to escape poverty. Many of these

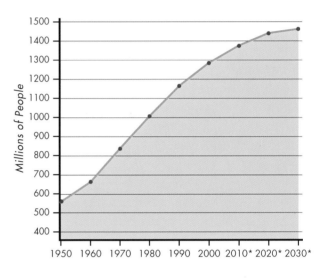

* Projected Population

▲ Population growth 1950-2030

workers travel from place to place, working on big engineering and building projects before moving on again. Thousands of women have moved from the rural areas of Sichuan to work in electronics factories in Guangdong Province in the southeast.

In 1950, only 12 per cent of the population lived in urban areas; in 2007, the figure was 42 per cent. China now has one hundred cities with a population exceeding one million, and by 2015, the majority of China's population is expected to be urban. Rapid urbanization and a big migratory workforce present the government with major problems. Cities are generally overcrowded, with families living in one or two rooms that are often rented from their employer. China's urban population is expected to grow by around 1.7 per cent per year up to 2025, as increasing numbers of rural residents turn to non-agricultural work to earn more and boost their standard of living.

Population data

- Population: 1,330 million
- Population 0-14 yrs: 20.1 per cent
- Population 15-64 yrs: 71.9 per cent
- Population 65+ yrs: 8 per cent
- Population growth rate: 0.6 per cent
- Population density: 138.6 per sq km/ 358.9 per sq mile
- Urban population: 42 per cent
- Major cities: Beijing 11,106,000
  Shanghai 14,978,000
  Tianjin 7,180,000

Source: United Nations and World Bank

Focus on: Shanghai

Shanghai started as a small, bustling fishing village at the mouth of the Yangtze River. It was one of the first Chinese ports to be opened up to foreign trade in the 19th century, and today has become China's biggest city. It has a registered population of 15 million, but it is estimated that there are at least five million unregistered, migrant workers in the city. Although the city has a negative birth rate, the number of migrants moving from rural areas is set to increase the city's population rapidly. One proposal to house Shanghai's growing population is the construction of a 300-storey skyscraper, reaching 1,128 m (3,700 feet) into the sky and accommodating 100,000 people. If it was built, it would be the world's tallest building.

▶ New apartment buildings in the district of Pudong, Shanghai, tower over the ramshackle houses that these people call home.

CHAPTER 5

Government and Politics

Since 1949, the Communist party has ruled China. The basic goal of the Communist state is to provide the 'iron rice bowl' – welfare for all, from the cradle to the grave. For decades, China's government tried to provide the iron rice bowl using a totalitarian system.

▲ The Chinese National People's Congress (the Chinese parliament) opens at the Great Hall of the People in Beijing, March 2004.

THE WORK UNIT

The Communist government still has representatives in the army, universities and in workplaces. From the 1950s, every Chinese adult was a member of a *danwei* – a work unit. Each *danwei* was managed by a member of the Communist party and it had great power over the day-to-day lives of its members including allocating housing, providing healthcare and education, and giving permission to travel away from home. However, with the introduction of economic reforms after 1978, the role of the *danwei* has become much weaker, particularly as employment has become increasingly flexible.

HUMAN RIGHTS ISSUES

The Chinese government places severe restrictions on freedom of speech, the media, religion and workers' rights. Dissidents who speak out against the Communist government are often imprisoned or forced to go and live in exile. Many dissidents have been put in prison for crimes such as petitioning for government reform, organizing workers, worshipping outside state-controlled venues, or using the Internet to call for government reform (see page 41).

In 1989, a massive student demonstration for democratic reform began in Tiananmen Square in Beijing. People from all walks of life joined the students. When the protesters demanded that the country's leadership resign, the government answered by sending in troops to repress the demonstration. It is estimated that up to 2,600 civilians were killed in the crackdown.

POLITICAL CHANGE

China's economic boom has resulted in huge differences in wealth between different parts of the country (see page 32). Some of the southern provinces, which have benefited most from economic reform, have challenged the authority of the central Communist government in Beijing. The outside world has seized on this opportunity to put pressure on China to uphold human rights, and to consider some degree of democratization as a way of holding together this vast country in the future.

Focus on: Challenging the state

Since 1949, the Chinese government has suppressed all forms of religion. Falun Gong is a spiritual movement based on Buddhist practices which started in China in the early 1990s. It quickly acquired millions of followers in China. However, the government was nervous of the threat to its authority posed by Falun Gong, and it banned the movement in 1999. Many Falun Gong leaders have been arrested and imprisoned.

Similarly, Tibetan Buddhist monks and nuns who refuse to denounce their religious leader, the Dalai Lama, have been arrested and imprisoned or expelled from China.

▼ Falun Gong followers demonstrate against the Chinese government in Hong Kong, April 2001. Although Falun Gong is banned in mainland China, it remains legal in Hong Kong.

INTERNAL STRUGGLES

Throughout its history China has gained and lost land. Originally, it covered the region around the Huang He (Yellow River). Since that time it has expanded in all directions and was at its largest during the T'ang (618-907), Yuan (1279-1368) and Ch'ing (1644-1911) dynasties. But as a result of various wars and disputes, some geographical areas remain in conflict today.

▼ The exiled Tibetan leader, the Dalai Lama, greets his followers during a visit to a Buddhist monastery in Calcutta, India, in September 2001.

TIBET

Tibet is a region of Central Asia and the home of the Tibetan people. Chinese troops invaded Tibet in 1950, forcing the Tibetan government, led by the Dalai Lama, to go into exile in northern India. While the Tibetan government still claims sovereignty over Tibet, China claims that Tibet has always been part of its territory. In 1965, Tibet became an autonomous region of China, with Xizang Zizhiqu (*zizhiqu* means 'autonomous region') as its Chinese name. Since 1989, the Chinese government has supported the systematic settlement of Han Chinese in Tibet. So many Han Chinese have been moved to Tibet that they threaten to outnumber the indigenous Tibetans, further diminishing any chances of Tibetan political independence.

SPECIAL ADMINISTRATIVE REGIONS

At the end of the First Opium War, Britain forced China to cede Hong Kong Island (see page 11). More territories were added under later treaties, but in 1997 the whole colony reverted to China. In 1984, Britain and China came to a compromise agreement which resulted in Hong Kong becoming a Special Administrative Region (SAR) of China. Under this agreement, China promised that it would not impose its Communist economic system on Hong Kong, and that Hong Kong would retain its independence in all matters apart from defence and foreign affairs. This agreement will last

▲ Hong Kong harbour at night, seen from the steep slopes of Victoria Peak on Hong Kong Island. Hong Kong has maintained its economic success since the handover to China in 1997.

until 2034. Until then Hong Kong has its own elected government, separate membership of international organizations, and its own currency (the Hong Kong dollar).

China's other SAR is Macao, also on the south coast, which was a Portuguese colony from 1887. It was handed back to China in 1999 under a similar compromise agreement to Hong Kong's, which guaranteed 'one country, two systems' for fifty years.

TAIWAN

In 1683, the island of Taiwan became part of the Ch'ing Empire. Officially, this island off China's southeast coast is still part of China, but it broke away from mainland control in 1949 when the defeated Nationalist government fled to Taiwan (see page 12). Taiwan has thrived as a free market economy and, along with Hong Kong, has given China a model for how it may develop economically in the future. While Taiwan has its own democratically elected government and is independent of China, the Chinese government still claims that Taiwan is under Chinese rule and refuses to have diplomatic relations with any country that recognizes Taiwan as a separate nation. However, although the United States withdrew formal recognition from Taiwan in 1979, when it recognized the People's Republic of China, it still adopts the two-China approach, ensuring Taiwan's security while insisting that there will be no military action by Taiwan against China.

CHAPTER 6

Energy and Resources

China has abundant natural resources, including massive energy resources and large reserves of minerals, timber and water. According to figures released in 2003 by the Chinese government, China has reserves of 158 different minerals, and is third in the world in terms of its total quantity of mineral reserves.

ENERGY SOURCES

China is the world's biggest producer and consumer of coal. Chinese coal accounts for over 40 per cent of all the coal mined in the world, and coal provides 63 per cent of China's total energy requirements. China also has substantial reserves of oil, estimated by a Chinese oil expert at 15.5 billion tonnes (15 billion tons), or about 1.3 per cent of the world's total reserves. However China's domestic consumption of oil is projected to reach 305 million tonnes (300 million tons) by 2010, by which time China will have to import half of its oil supplies. There are vast untapped reserves of oil and natural gas in the Tarim Basin – an area the size of France in Xinjiang Province, in the far west of the country. Gas production in this region started in 2005, and gas is pumped through a west-east pipeline, 4,200 km (2,610 miles) to the east of the country.

One important alternative to using fossil fuels such as coal, oil and gas as a source of energy is hydroelectric power (HEP). Many of China's rivers flow through steep-sided valleys, providing the ideal conditions for building

▼ Rescuers help a worker out of a coal mine at Benxi, in the northeastern province of Liaoning, after the mine flooded in March 2002.

dams and harnessing the power of the water for HEP. However, although HEP is a much more environmentally friendly source of energy than coal or oil, it has its drawbacks. The controversial Three Gorges Dam project on the Yangtze River has seen the construction of the world's largest dam, 2 km (1.2 miles) in length and 185 m (607 feet) high. The reservoir behind the dam will cover 632 sq km (244 sq miles), but

▼ Water gushes through the open sluice gates of the massive Three Gorges Dam on the Yangtze River.

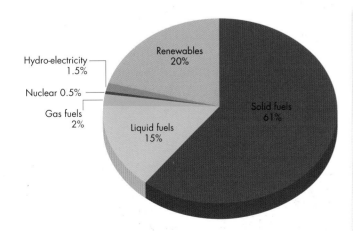

Hydro-electricity 1.5%
Nuclear 0.5%
Gas fuels 2%
Liquid fuels 15%
Solid fuels 61%
Renewables 20%

▲ Energy generation by source

Energy data

- Energy consumption as percentage of world total: 11.3 per cent
- Energy consumption by sector (percentage of total): Industry: 42, Transportation: 11 Agriculture: 4, Services: 4, Residential: 39
- CO_2 emissions as percentage of world total: 17.3
- CO_2 emissions per capita in tonnes p.a.: 3.8

Source: World Resources Institute

its creation has flooded a vast area of agricultural land and submerged the homes of more than a million people. The project was started in 1993 and is due to be completed in 2009, when all 26 generators will be able to generate enough power to supply one-ninth of China's total electricity production.

ENERGY CONSUMPTION

Demand for energy is rising rapidly in China, and is outstripping supply. China's energy consumption per person grew by about 100 per cent between 1980 and 2004 – ten times more than the increase in energy consumption in the UK in the same period. What's more, China's energy consumption is projected to grow by another 100 per cent between 2004 and 2015.

In 2008, China was the world's second largest consumer (after the United States) of petroleum products. Its consumption of oil is now larger than its production, so China imports petroleum products from the Middle East and Russia. Coal is also vitally important in China's economic development. Between 1971 and 1996 the demand for coal increased five-fold, with alarming consequences for the environment because of the increase in mining. By 2004, however, improved energy efficiency, environmental regulations and new energy sources had slowed down the use of coal a little. Nuclear plants have also been developed as a 'cleaner' way of producing energy.

WATER RESOURCES

China has two of the world's longest rivers, the Yangtze and the Huang He (Yellow River). Water is crucial to China's industry and farming, as well as being needed for domestic use. Although China is the fifth richest nation in water resources (after Brazil, Russia, Canada and the United States), its reserves are very unevenly distributed. While there are ample

▼ A villager washes her vegetables at a communal tap in Shiqing, Guizhou Province, southeast China.

water supplies south of the Yangtze River, parts of China north of the Yangtze have severe water shortages. The South-to-North Water Transfer Project (see box below) aims to address this problem.

MINERAL RESOURCES

China has a wide range of important mineral resources. Most of China's minerals are found in the northeast and central parts of the country. They include titanium, a rare and valuable metal used in joint-replacement surgery, and tungsten which is used in the manufacture of light bulbs. China is also a major producer of tin, antimony, zinc, molybdenum, lead and mercury, as well as ferrous metals such as iron, manganese and vanadium.

FISHING

China is the world's largest fishing nation with a catch of around 43 million tonnes (42.3 million tons) per year. Fish such as hairtail, chub mackerel and black scraper are found in the vast coastal fisheries in the Bohai, Yellow, East China and South China seas. Inland freshwater fisheries are also important for species such as carp, trout and salmon.

▲ This fisherman is using two cormorants to catch fish, a traditional method of fishing. The picture was taken in 2000 on the Li River in Guangxi Province.

 Did you know?

Of the 45,000 large dams in the world (over 17 m (50 feet) high), more than 22,000 are in China.

Focus on: The South-to-North Water Transfer Project

In December 2002, China began a gigantic south-to-north water diversion project, which is expected to take fifty years to complete, and cost US$59 billion. The main aim of the project is to alleviate the water shortages in northern China, particularly around Beijing, Tianjin and in Hubei Province, by diverting water from the south of the country. The project involves building three canals to carry water to the drought-ridden areas. The canals will cross the eastern, middle and western parts of China, linking the country's four major rivers – the Yangtze, the Huang He (Yellow River), the Huai He and the Hai He. Critics of this massive scheme are concerned about how it may damage the environment in the area where the water originates. They argue that the solution to China's water problems lies not in moving water, but in measures such as water conservation and improved irrigation efficiency.

CHAPTER 7

Economy and Income

After the death of Mao Zedong, and the victory of the reformers (see page 13), China began to modernize its economy. Since 1978, China has gone from being a centrally controlled economy dominated by state-owned industry to an economy in which the market is determined by the supply and demand of goods.

THE OPEN-DOOR POLICY

It was Deng Xiaoping who started the transformation of China's economy. Before 1978, China's main trading partners were the USSR and other Communist states, and its economy was centrally planned and tightly controlled by the Communist government. Over the following years, China encouraged foreign investment in order to provide the money to build new businesses, and to bring in new technology – the so-called Open-Door Policy. In 1980, direct foreign investment in China totalled US$6,251 million. By 2006, this figure had risen to US$602,650 million.

Most of China's economic growth has been focused in the southern part of the country. Since 1980, five special economic zones (SEZs) have been set up along the south coast: Shenzhen, Zhuhai and Shantou in Guangdong Province, Xiamen in Fujian Province, and the island province of Hainan. These SEZs were established to encourage foreign businesses to invest in China through preferential tax policies and other incentives, and to be centres of science and industry. In 1984, the Communist

Economic data

- Gross National Income (GNI) in US$: 3,120,891,000,000
- World rank by GNI: 4
- GNI per capita in US$: 2,360
- World rank by GNI per capita: 132
- Economic growth: 11.4 per cent

Source: World Bank

◀ Chinese workers assemble DVD players for export to the United States and Europe at a factory in Zhenjiang, Jiangxi Province, in eastern China.

government also created a coastal zone of 'open' cities where foreign investment was permitted and encouraged, reaching from Dalian in the north to Zhanjiang and Beihai in the south. This 'open' zone has since been extended further, with particular success in the Pudong New Zone in Shanghai, which has attracted many foreign-funded banks and businesses. By 2008, the number of special economic zones and open cities had reached 28 as part of China's continued policy to attract foreign investment.

EXTERNAL AND INTERNAL MARKETS

In the five years up to 2002, Chinese exports increased by more than 50 per cent to US$325 billion, and have since nearly tripled to US$1,213 billion in 2007. China mainly exports to the United States (19 per cent), Hong Kong (15 per cent), Japan (8 per cent), South Korea (5 per cent) and Germany (4 per cent), although the huge range of goods that it produces are found all over the world. Many of these products are high-tech electronic goods such as DVD players, mobile phones or flat-screen monitors, but China is also a major exporter of clothing and textiles, toys and sports goods, minerals and foodstuffs.

In the boom areas of the south and east, some Chinese people have themselves become important new consumers, with vastly increased spending-power. Mobile phones and cars are particularly popular consumer items in China, and it is estimated that in 2005, one in every three people in China will own a

▼ Chinese consumers inspect new cars at the 'All in Auto 2004' exhibition in Shanghai. For those people in China who can afford them, large, expensive cars are important status symbols.

 Did you know?

The world's largest shoe factory is in Guangdong Province. It employs 80,000 people.

mobile phone. Although the proportion of the 'new rich' is very small, China's population is so vast that even if only 1 per cent of people can afford a car, that still represents a potential market of 13 million people. Today, car ownership in China is rising dramatically, with the car sector growing by about 22 per cent a year (at a time when the automobile industry in Europe and the United States is growing by only 2 per cent).

UNEMPLOYMENT

Until the 1990s, unemployment did not exist in China. But as the country has shifted increasingly to a market economy, many Chinese people have found themselves out of work. China's unemployment rate is officially about 4 per cent, although this takes into account only urban unemployment. In 1999 and 2000, State-owned Enterprises (SOEs) were still the greatest providers of jobs in China. But as increasing numbers of inefficient SOEs have been closed by the government, many former employees have been unable to find alternative work. There are also millions of 'surplus' unskilled, rural labourers, who are not included in the official unemployment figures.

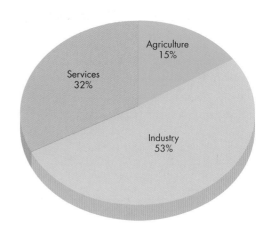

▲ Economy by sector

THE WEALTH GAP

Despite China's impressive economic growth, the vast majority of Chinese people still live in poverty. Most people in rural China have not experienced the benefits of the economic boom, and millions have migrated to the cities and industrialized areas seeking work and better wages. In the two decades between 1984 and 2004, more than 200 million people moved to

▼ A water buffalo is used to pull a plough in Guizhou Province, southern China.

▶ Loading shopping bags in the car park of the new IKEA home goods store in Beijing.

the cities to look for work. By 2024, another 300 million migrants are expected to join them. The wealth gap between urban and rural China is a direct result of the country's overall economic success. In 2006, the average income for an urban worker in China was US$2,009 while for rural workers it was less than a third of this amount – US$608. The Chinese government recognizes that this growing inequality between rich and poor is one of the major challenges for the future, and has pledged to spend billions of dollars to raise farmers' incomes.

WORKERS' RIGHTS

In China, it is illegal for workers to organize independent unions or to strike, and protests against unfair conditions are strongly suppressed by the Communist government. Furthermore, while Chinese labour law provides strong protection for workers' rights, these laws are often poorly enforced. Violations such as forced labour, child labour, excessive overtime, substandard wages and hazardous working conditions are commonplace. The average income for most workers remains low, and China still ranks as a poor country by international measures.

 Did you know?

Eleven out of every 1,000 Chinese workers die annually from industrial accidents.

Focus on: The Pearl River delta

The Pearl River delta consists of Hong Kong, Macao and Guangdong Province. Twenty-five years ago, farmland and small rural villages dominated this area; today it is one of the fastest growing regions in China. More than half the world's population is within five hours' flying time of Hong Kong, making the SAR (see page 24) an attractive economic centre. In recent years, many Hong Kong industries have moved on to mainland China, fuelling massive economic growth. Shenzhen in Guangdong Province was also China's first special economic zone (see page 30). It is now the world's top exporter of watches, telephones, radios, toys, footwear and clothing, and is being marketed as China's science and technology city of the future.

CHAPTER 8

Global Connections

Throughout most of the 20th century China was isolated from the rest of the world, which saw China as being remote and inward-looking. But since the late 1970s, reforms introduced by the Communist government have opened up the country to the outside world, particularly in the area of trade, free markets and foreign investments. Despite its own abundance of natural resources, China still needs to import huge amounts of raw materials from other countries to fulfil the needs of its manufacturing industries.

COMPETING WITH THE WORLD

China strengthened its entry into the global market by joining the World Trade Organization (WTO) in 2001. The aim of this organization is to make trade easier between member countries, and entry into the WTO has required China's Communist government to introduce more reforms, such as the reduction of tariffs on imported goods and allowing more foreign access to its huge internal market.

The main attraction for many foreign companies setting up in China has been the low cost of production, based on low wages and tax breaks given by the Chinese government. Some people have complained that

◄ The China World Trade Center in Beijing opened for business in 1990 and is marketed as 'the place where China meets the world'.

these incentives give companies in China unfair advantages, as manufacturers in Western countries are unable to compete with China's prices. But businesses around the world are increasingly buying their goods from Chinese suppliers or moving their factory work to China to take advantage of the cheaper costs.

China is now the world's largest consumer of many industrial commodities and raw materials. Its surge in demand for raw materials has benefited some countries, for example China's demand for leather, for its shoe factories, has revived the leather industry in Brazil. However, China's booming demand for oil has been a major reason for the increase in global oil prices since 2004. To ensure access to the resources it needs, China is increasingly investing in other countries. For example, the China National Petroleum Company has invested US$700 million in Kazakhstan to secure future supplies of oil.

GLOBAL RELATIONSHIPS

China recognizes the importance of establishing good relationships with other countries for its future prosperity and security, particularly the United States. It is one of only five permanent members of the United Nations Security Council (the branch of the UN that maintains peace and security between nations). Under the Nuclear Non-Proliferation Treaty, the five permanent members are the only countries in the world permitted to possess nuclear weapons. Since North Korea admitted in 2002 that it had been developing nuclear weapons in defiance of the treaty, China has supported a nuclear-free Korean peninsula and has played an important diplomatic role mediating between the United States and North Korea.

THE CHINESE ABROAD

China has a long history of trading with other countries. For thousands of years, silk was exported along the 'Silk Road', the overland trade route that linked China with countries to the west. Many Chinese merchants moved to Southeast Asia and large Chinese settlements were created in Java, Malaya, Vietnam, Thailand, Singapore and the Philippines. But during the 18th and 19th centuries, China became increasingly isolated from the rest of the world (see pages 10-11).

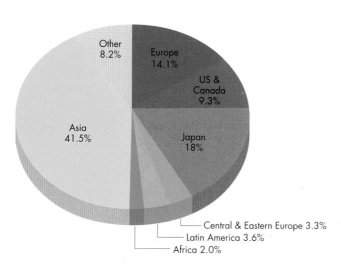

▲ Import origins as percentage of world total

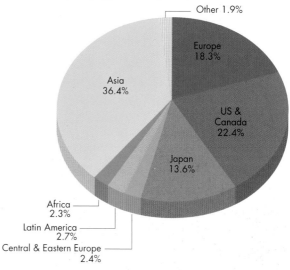

▲ Export destinations as percentage of world total

▲ A wooden bus with open sides like a tram takes passengers beneath a Chinese-style bridge in Chinatown, San Francisco, USA. There are thriving Chinese communities in many major cities around the world.

During the 19th and large parts of the 20th century, China's isolationism was a deliberate attempt to prevent the spread of Western influence within its borders. The Chinese government imposed strict controls to prevent people from leaving the country, but despite these restrictions many people escaped, fleeing famine, poverty or war for better lives elsewhere. By 1854, an estimated 2,400 Chinese were in Australia working in the gold mines. By 1857, the number had risen to 25,424. It is estimated that over 25,000 Chinese people took part in the California Gold Rush in the United States in 1852.

Many of these emigrants were unable to return to China and settled overseas. Cities such as San Francisco, New York, Vancouver and Toronto in North America; Sydney, Melbourne and Brisbane in Australia; and London in the UK, all have a 'Chinatown' – an area full of Chinese shops and restaurants. Today there are over 3 million Chinese people living in the United States, over 670,000 in Australia and around 350,000 in the UK.

HUMAN TRAFFICKING

The desire to move abroad is still strong amongst many Chinese people, but the Chinese government continues to impose restrictions on leaving the country, and on entry to many other countries. As a result, an illegal trade in human beings has developed. People are enticed by stories of better lives abroad to pay large sums of money to so-called 'snakeheads'. For around US$12,000, a huge amount of money in China, these 'snakeheads' arrange for people to be smuggled out, most frequently to Japan or the UK. Wages in the UK, even in illegal employment, are ten times what a Chinese worker could earn at home. Once settled and working, Chinese immigrants often send large amounts of money back to their families in China, making significant contributions to household incomes.

CULTURAL CONTRIBUTIONS

As Chinese people have settled abroad, they have taken their own ways of life with them. Some aspects of Chinese culture have become very well-known all over the globe. Chinese cooking is recognized as one of the great cuisines of the world, and has been extremely influential. Martial arts such as *tai chi* and *kung fu* have become very popular in the West. Chinese ideas about design and style have also had a major impact, particularly ideas based on the ancient Chinese science of *Feng Shui* (literally, 'wind,

water'). *Feng Shui* uses the theory that an energy flows through and around us, and that balancing this energy by arranging objects in certain ways is important to a healthy and successful life. Such ideas have become increasingly popular in the West in the last twenty years.

▼ Vancouver in Canada has a large Chinese population and parts of the city cater specifically for this community. This Chinese supermarket is in the city's Chinatown district.

Focus on: The illegal trade in humans

In June 2000, fifty-eight out of a group of sixty Chinese immigrants were discovered dead in an airtight container when a lorry that had just crossed the English Channel from Zeebrugge arrived in the British port of Dover. Each of the would-be immigrants had paid US$20,000 to a 'snakehead' to smuggle them into Britain, and had travelled for weeks via Yugoslavia, Hungary, Austria, France and the Netherlands. Before leaving the Netherlands, the lorry driver had closed the air-vent to avoid his human cargo being spotted at immigration checks. When dock workers at Dover searched the container, they found that only two of the group were still alive.

CHAPTER 9

Transport and Communications

China is struggling to modernize its infrastructure. Its transport system is under great pressure to cope with its fast-growing economy, its huge population, and the vast distances across the country. As people become wealthier there is an increasing demand for cars as well as a need for more efficient forms of transport to help open up poorer, inland areas.

▼ Passengers board a domestic flight at Beijing Capital International Airport. Air travel has become increasingly important as China's economy has developed, and China now has the fastest growing air transport market in the world.

TRANSPORT INFRASTRUCTURE

Like everything else in China, the transport networks are growing at a dramatic rate. There is an urgent need to modernize and expand the country's transport systems to take raw materials to factories and manufactured goods to the cities and ports. Rivers and waterways carry about a third of all China's internal freight, while the rail network carries fifty per cent. The Chinese railway system is run and largely funded by the government. Development of the railway system is a priority, and future plans include the construction of China's first-ever express passenger service, linking the cities of Beijing and Tianjin,

opened in 2008. Other similar lines are planned for the Yangtze delta and the Pearl River delta.

Air transport is very important in a country as large as China. There are major international airports at Beijing, Shanghai and Hong Kong, and over 300 smaller airports with paved runways. Many airports have been rebuilt and enlarged, and small airlines are growing rapidly. When it comes to roads the difference between the urban and rural areas is stark. A motorway network links the main cities, and there are now five ring roads around the capital, Beijing, to cope with the city's congested traffic. Yet many rural communities are not served by roads, and remain inaccessible.

▲ Smog envelops the city as vehicles crawl along a major road in Beijing. China committed to improving its air quality before the Olympic Games, which it hosted in 2008.

Transport & communications data

- 🗀 Total roads: 1,930,544 km/ 1,199,584 miles
- 🗀 Total paved roads: 1,575,571 km/ 979,014 miles
- 🗀 Total unpaved roads: 354,973 km/ 220,570 miles
- 🗀 Total railways: 75,438 km/ 46,875 miles
- 🗀 Airports: 403
- 🗀 Cars per 1,000 people: 24
- 🗀 Mobile phones per 1,000 people: 411
- 🗀 Personal computers per 1,000 people: 60
- 🗀 Internet users per 1,000 people: 190

Source: World Bank and CIA World Factbook

 Did you know?

China has built enough roads since 1990 to loop 16 times round the equator (approximately 640,000 km; 400,000 miles).

Focus on: Railway to Lhasa

Some areas of China still remain remote and inaccessible. The city of Lhasa in Tibet was once only reachable by air. The government has now built a 1,140-km (708-mile) railway to link the city with the rest of China. Opened in 2006, it is the highest altitude railway in the world, and cuts across vast areas of grassland, lakes and mountains. Concerns have been raised about the impact the project will have on the environment. While the railway will bring jobs to this remote area, many Tibetans see this improvement in communications as another way in which China is increasing its political control over them.

PERSONAL TRANSPORT

There are 300 million bicycles in China, and they are still the most common form of personal transport in the country. But the familiar image of China's city streets filled with bicycles is changing. In 1990 there were only one million cars in the country; by 2005 there were thirty times this number. However, despite this rise in car ownership, only 24 out of every 1,000 Chinese people have a car – compared to 814 out of every 1,000 people in the United States.

THE CHINESE MEDIA

The Chinese government is heavily involved in all aspects of the media – newspapers, TV and radio, and the Internet – and there are many restrictions on what is written or broadcast. However, the changes that are taking place as China turns to a more open, market economy are making it increasingly difficult for its government to control the media as tightly as in the past.

THE INTERNET

The use of the Internet is a good example of the dilemma faced by the Chinese government. While government officials want to encourage Chinese people to keep up with and use the latest Internet technology, they also want to control the information available to people in China on the Web. China now has more than 250 million Internet surfers, the second largest number in the world after the United States. However, a large percentage of these Internet users are located in the major cities and in the coastal commercial centres, while only a tiny proportion of people in the undeveloped rural areas in the west have access to the Internet.

▼ Chinese officials confiscate computers from an illegal Internet café in Shunde, southern China, in January 2004. Since 2001, the Chinese government has tightened its control on Internet cafés throughout the country.

Many people in China use Internet cafés to access the World Wide Web, but in recent years the government has closed down thousands of these cafés for failing to abide by the strict laws concerning the services they can provide. The Chinese government also blocks access to many foreign websites, and requires some Internet service providers (ISPs) to record details of the people who use their websites. While search engines such as Google do operate in China, information about 'forbidden' subjects such as Tibet, the SARS virus (see page 44), or the banned religious group Falun Gong is blocked by the government.

Despite these restrictions, closer contact with the West through travel and business as well as the media is increasingly influencing the opinions of many young and educated people in China. Television satellite dishes are able to pick up programmes from Hong Kong and Taiwan, and China now has the biggest market in the world for mobile phones.

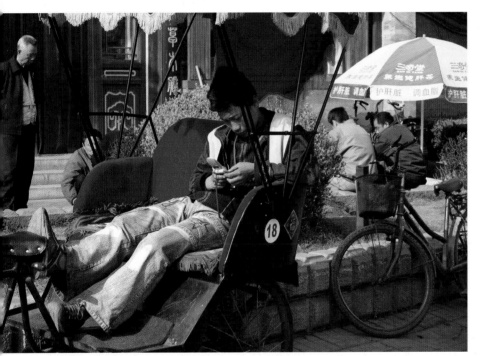

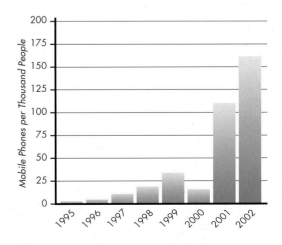

◄ A young rickshaw driver in Beijing sends text messages to his friends on his mobile phone as he waits for his next customer.

Focus on: Texting

Text messaging has become very popular in China, particularly as it is impossible to censor. During the SARS epidemic of 2002-3 (see page 44) the government imposed a strict media blackout. Many Chinese people first heard about the virus through their mobile phones. A text message 'There is a fatal flu in Guangzhou' was sent over 120 million times in three days. As a direct result of texting, the government was forced to admit the existence of the virus.

▲ Mobile phone use, 1995-2002

CHAPTER 10

Education and Health

The Chinese education and health systems are controlled and run by the government. However, China struggles to educate and provide adequate health facilities for its 1.3 billion people.

▲ A class in a rural school in central China. In addition to Chinese, these children will learn to read and write at least one foreign language, most likely English. In contrast, their parents were lucky if they learned how to read and write in Chinese.

EDUCATION FOR ALL

Providing education for its vast population is a huge challenge for the Chinese government. Nevertheless, much of China's population is well-educated. One-child couples pin a lot of hope on their only child doing well in school, passing exams and getting a good job so that he or she can support them in later life. Since 1986, attendance at school has been compulsory for at least nine years. Children are expected to work

hard, and even primary-school-age children often have several hours of homework every night. Going to school is taken for granted by almost all school-aged children in the country's cities and towns. But in poor, rural areas, some students struggle to stay in school because of financial problems. There are fees for all levels of education in China. Even the official media admit that as many as five million children between the ages of seven and eleven do not go to school because their parents simply cannot afford it.

In many schools, class sizes are large – with up to 50 or 60 pupils – and the school day is long – starting at 7a.m. and finishing after 5p.m. Students often take additional courses during the holidays. Every student is required

Education and health

- Life expectancy at birth male: 71.4
- Life expectancy at birth female: 75.2
- Infant mortality rate per 1,000: 21
- Under five mortality rate per 1,000: 24
- Physicians per 1,000 people: 2
- Health expenditure as percentage of GDP: 4.7 per cent
- Education expenditure as percentage of GDP: 1.9 per cent
- Primary net enrolment: 93 per cent
- Pupil-teacher ratio, primary: 18
- Adult literacy as percentage age 15+: 90.9

Source: United Nations Agencies and World Bank

to learn English as well as Chinese. Partly because of the need to learn large numbers of complex Chinese characters, schools often adopt rote-learning, requiring students to memorize their lessons. However, in 2004 the government stated that it wanted education to encourage children to think more for themselves and become what it described as 'well-rounded citizens' – a direct result of the move towards a more business-oriented society and the need for people who are both creative and flexible.

HIGHER EDUCATION

In a country of 1.3 billion people, there are only 2.5 million university places and competition for them is intense. China has failed to expand its university and college enrolment adequately because its public expenditure on education is one of the lowest in the world, despite the government's stated commitment to education. China is ranked 119th out of 130 countries in terms of the amount it spends per capita on education – half the level of spending on education in developed countries.

Loans and scholarships are available to fund university education. Although many students are assigned jobs once they graduate, some graduates are now permitted to choose their jobs. Internet-based, long-distance learning has become increasingly popular since it was first introduced in 1998.

▲ Two medical students from Mongolia pose proudly in front of their university motto, outside a university building in Xi'an, central China. They will be some of the first doctors to qualify from their villages.

Focus on: School funding

In 2001 a massive explosion killed at least 37 children and four teachers in a rural primary school in Fang Lin village, Jiangxi, one of China's poorest provinces. It was later discovered that the school was using pupils as young as eight years old to assemble fireworks to boost its income.

Funding shortages have often prompted schools to seek alternative ways of generating income. Many schools in China hire out their students as cheap labour to increase the school's income, particularly in rural areas where schools receive less government funding.

HEALTH CARE

After the founding of the People's Republic of China, a health system was set up to provide basic care that was free and widely available. As a result, life expectancy in China increased from 35 years in 1949 to 65 years in the mid-1970s. But since the introduction of economic reforms in the late 1970s, a big gap has opened up in the provision of health care between urban and rural areas.

The leading causes of death in China are similar to those in the West – cancer and heart disease. Through country-wide campaigns to improve sanitation and hygiene, epidemic diseases such as cholera, scarlet fever and typhoid have almost been eradicated. But tuberculosis (TB) – a disease that is now virtually unknown in developed countries – still accounts for thousands of deaths every year in China, mainly in rural areas.

DIFFERENCES IN CARE

Life expectancy in China is now 71 years for men, 75 years for women. However, these statistics conceal the huge differences between health care in urban and rural areas in China. The move towards a market economy (see page 30) during the 1980s caused the old systems for funding health care to break down. As clinics and hospitals ran out of money, they began to charge patients for treatment and medicines. For the majority of people in the wealthier urban areas, these costs could be covered by health insurance. But in the poor, rural areas, where few people have such insurance, millions of people cannot afford even the most basic medical attention. The whole system is under strain and in an emergency, such as the outbreak of SARS in 2002, it struggles to cope.

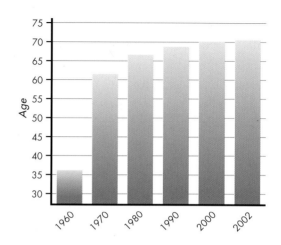

▲ Life expectancy at birth 1960-2002

SARS

An outbreak of severe acute respiratory syndrome (SARS) started in Guangdong Province in southern China in November 2002. It quickly spread to Hong Kong, and to other parts of mainland China, including the capital Beijing. In April 2003 the Chinese government was forced to apologize for its slow response to the disease, which spread all around the world. The threat of SARS caused the city authorities in Beijing to close down schools, theatres, cinemas and bars to try to contain the disease. SARS killed 349 people in China in 2003.

TRADITIONAL MEDICINE

Although many Chinese medical professionals practise Western medicine, many people in China still use traditional Chinese medicine. Sometimes doctors use a combination of

 Did you know?

The Chinese smoke 30 per cent of the world's cigarettes. It is estimated that 200 million Chinese men smoke, and that half of this number could die from tobacco-related diseases before 2030.

Western and traditional Chinese treatments. The theory behind traditional Chinese medicine is that dynamic energy – *qi* – runs in channels, called meridians, through the body. Illness occurs when the meridians become blocked. Chinese medicine aims to maintain or restore harmony in the body using acupuncture, herbal medicine and massage. Traditional Chinese medicine uses thousands of plant species as well as animal parts, and China has about 250,000 doctors trained in traditional medicine, although there are also thousands of 'unofficial' practitioners.

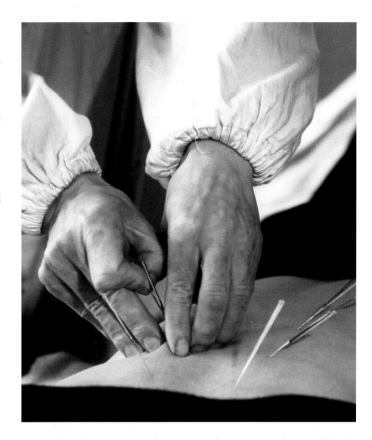

▶ A patient receives acupunture treatment in a hospital in Chengdu, Sichuan Province, central China. Acupuncture involves piercing certain points of the body with thin needles.

Focus on: HIV/AIDS in China

There are around 700,000 people living with HIV/AIDS in China today, but overall the HIV/AIDS epidemic is stabilizing. Although this figure is small as a proportion of the country's total population, many people in certain population groups are still becoming infected. Many people have caught the virus through intravenous drug use or prostitution. In some rural areas, poor workers have contracted the virus from unsterilized equipment after selling their blood to illegal blood banks. The Chinese government denied that there was a problem until 2001, when it finally admitted that the country was facing a serious crisis. Since then, the HIV/AIDS Action Plan for China 2006-2010 has been spreading information and improving testing and treatment.

▶ Commuters in Nanyang, Henan Province, look at adverts on the grab-handles in a bus. The crossed red ribbon is an international symbol for AIDS awareness.

CHAPTER 11

Culture and Religion

During the Cultural Revolution (see page 13), Mao Zedong exhorted the Chinese to turn their backs on the 'four olds' – old ideas, culture, custom and habits. Today, China's rich cultural heritage is once again acknowledged and celebrated.

THE FAMILY

The idea of the family is very important in China. Several generations of one family often live together, and the elderly are respected and cared for by their relatives. However, these traditional values are changing. Divorce is on the increase and 14 per cent of households now consist of either a single adult, or a childless couple who both work.

▼ A family reunion in Henan Province, 2002. The family sits around a table together to eat a traditional meal. The food is placed on a revolving platform in the centre of the table, so that each person may help themselves to a little of each dish.

FOOD

Chinese food varies considerably from region to region. In the north of the country, where wheat is the staple crop, meals are based on noodles. In the south, rice is the staple food. Rice is eaten so regularly in the southern regions that a common greeting is "Have you eaten rice yet?". There are four main styles of regional cuisine. Cantonese cooking (from Guangdong Province) uses stir-frying and steaming as the main methods of cooking fresh ingredients. In the cold north, wheat noodles, dumplings and steamed breads are basic foods. Peking (Beijing) duck and Mongolian hot-pot are popular dishes. Food from China's largest province, Sichuan, is characterized by spices and chilli peppers, with dishes such as hot and

▲ Street vendors prepare their food in Urumqi, Xinjiang Province, in the northwest of China. The food is cooked and kept hot over a brazier.

sour soup. The cuisine of eastern China is based on rice, and sugar is used to sweeten many of its rich dishes. All over China, people eat from bowls with chopsticks. Stalls selling snacks such as kebabs, noodles or dumplings are found on the streets of the larger cities.

 Did you know?

China's three most popular surnames – Li, Wang and Zhang – belong to over 280 million Chinese, almost the same number of people as live in the USA.

RELIGION AND COMMUNISM

Throughout China's history, the three main religions in the country have been Taoism, Confucianism and Buddhism. After 1949, the Communists discouraged the practice of any religion, closed down monasteries and converted many temples to other uses. During the Cultural Revolution, religion was attacked as part of China's 'old' culture. This situation eased when the reformers came to power in 1978 (see page 13), but the Communist government still does not encourage religion and, officially, China is an atheist country. However, in order to improve relations with some of its minority groups, and as a result of pressure from outside China, the government now allows more freedom to practise religion.

RELIGIONS IN CHINA

Taoism is a native Chinese religion and its founder, Laozi, is said to have lived during the

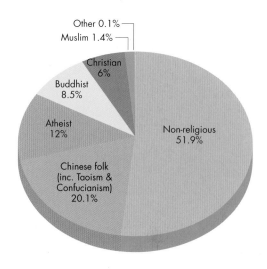

▲ China's major religions

6th century BC. One of its fundamental teachings is that people are part of the wider environment and that there is no such thing as 'self'. The philosophies of Confucius (see page 9) emphasize the importance of the family and order in society. Buddhism came to China from India as early as the first century AD. It is estimated that up to 100 million Chinese follow the Buddhist religion. Despite having been suppressed, these belief systems continue to have a major influence on the way Chinese people behave and think.

Western missionaries brought Christianity to China in the 17th century, although it is possible that Christians visited China as early as the 5th century. The number of Christians in China today is estimated at 79 million. Contacts between the Islamic world and China started in the 7th century. The T'ang emperor Yung-Wei approved the establishment of the first Chinese mosque at Ch'ang-an (Xi'an) – a building that still stands today. Unofficial estimates put the

▲ A Buddhist pilgrim spins prayer wheels mounted along a wall of the Potala Palace in Lhasa, Tibet. Buddhists believe that spinning the wheels releases their prayers.

Muslim population in China today at around 18 million. The main Muslim groups in the Chinese population are the Hui and the Uyghurs.

FESTIVALS

Festivals are a major part of Chinese life. The Chinese New Year is a big event and is celebrated with dragon and lion dances, and firecrackers. Another important festival is Ching Ming or 'Remembrance of Ancestors Day'. People visit their family tombs to clean them, and to leave food and offerings for the spirits of their ancestors.

The lion dance is performed at most Chinese festivals, particularly at Chinese New Year and at weddings. Two people perform the dance; one controls the highly decorated lion's head while the other moves the body and tail of the lion under a cloth attached to the head. The dance is believed to bring both happiness and good luck.

The Taoist Bun Festival is a spectacular festival that is unique to Cheung Chau, a small island in Hong Kong. Huge structures of bamboo are covered with bread buns. In the past, young people scrambled up the towers to grab as many buns as they could, but after several injuries in 1978, the buns are now handed out.

Kites are also an integral part of Chinese culture. They have special religious significance because they are seen as a means of making contact with the gods in heaven. It takes many years to become a master kite-maker, although most Chinese boys and girls learn to make their own kites at an early age. Weifang in Shandong Province is famous for its kite-making and-flying customs. Every April people come from all over the world to fly their kites in the annual kite festival which is held there.

▼ Chinese dancers perform the lion dance in a park in Beijing, February 2005. This ceremony marked the beginning of the Chinese New Year celebrations.

CHAPTER 12

Leisure and Tourism

Until the 1980s, weekends were unknown to most Chinese people. Most people's leisure time was restricted by the amount of work they had to do and the money they needed to earn, and working seven days a week in a factory or on a farm was common.

LEISURE TIME

The government introduced official, two-day weekends during the 1990s and most people now get two days off during the week. Since 1999 there have also been three week-long holidays in China, known as 'Golden Weeks' which are based around Chinese New Year in late January or early February, May Day, and National Day in October. These holidays have boosted the economy, as millions of Chinese spend money travelling to see relatives,

shopping and celebrating. However, many people dislike these 'fixed' holidays during which tourist destinations are crowded and prices are often inflated. It is possible that the Golden Weeks will be replaced with a more flexible system of holidays.

Older people, especially men, can be seen in street-side cafes and bars all over China, playing chess and cards. In particular, the clicking of tiles resounds through streets and alleyways as people play the popular game *mah jong*.

▼ *Tai chi* is popular throughout China, especially amongst the elderly. These participants are practising early in the morning in a park in Shanghai. *Tai chi* involves the co-ordination of mind, body and breathing in a series of slow, controlled movements.

SPORT

Martial arts (or *wushu*) were developed in China nearly 3,000 years ago as a form of self-defence and survival. They aim to improve physical ability, overall health and willpower and are now considered to be as much a sport as a way of fighting. Chinese martial arts include *karate*, *tai chi* and *kung fu*. It is often possible to see people doing *tai chi* in public parks early in the morning. *Tai chi* has been claimed to reduce stress levels and lower blood pressure.

Chinese people enjoy watching and playing many sports. Many of them excel at sports such as table tennis, badminton, basketball, snooker and golf. In addition, they are passionate about football and the national team reached the World Cup finals for the first time in 2002. China hosted the 2008 Olympic Games in Beijing, and won the most gold medals of any competing nation. Chinese sportsmen and women won 51 gold, 21 silver and 28 bronze medals, totaling 100. China was second only to the United States in the medals table.

? Did you know?

The Chinese basketball player Wang Zhizhi was the first Asian person to play in the American National Basketball Association. He was signed by the Dallas Mavericks in 2001. Other Chinese players who have played in the National Basketball Association are Yao Ming and Mengke Bateer.

▼ China's goalkeeper, Liu Yunfei, saves a goal during the Asian Cup football final against Japan in Beijing, August 2004. Japan eventually won 3–1.

TOURISM

Tourism is yet another growth industry in China with the numbers of foreign visitors rocketing from 710,000 in 1978 to 50 million by 2006. Most of these visitors come from China's near neighbours in Asia, such as Japan and Korea, and from Russia. Over 800,000 people from the United States and nearly 300,000 from the UK came to China in 2003. Many visitors to China are Chinese people who live in other countries, or business travellers, but an increasing number of tourists on luxury tours as well as independent backpackers also visit China. It is estimated that China will be the world's top tourist destination by 2020, with up to 130 million visitors a year.

In the past, the government did little to encourage visitors. Now, however, it recognizes that tourism is yet another way in which it can make money. Most of China, including Tibet, is open to foreign

Tourism in China

- 🗀 Tourist arrivals, millions: 49,000,000
- 🗀 Earnings from tourism in US$: 37,132,000,000
- 🗀 Tourism as percentage of foreign earnings: 3
- 🗀 Tourist departures, millions: 34,524,000
- 🗀 Expenditure on tourism in US$: 28,242,000,000

Source: World Bank

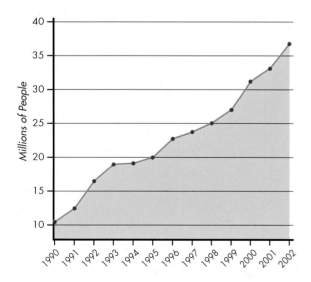

▲ Changes in international tourism, 1990-2002

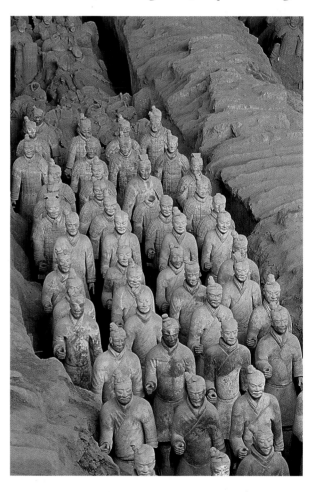

▲ The famous Terracotta Army, near Xi'an, central China, was discovered in 1974. It consists of more than 6,000 clay figures and horses in three burial pits which date back to the Qin dynasty (221-206 BC). Today, the Terracotta Army is one of China's main tourist attractions.

tourists, although access to some western areas is still restricted. The country has many historic and cultural attractions, including the Great Wall of China, the Forbidden City in Beijing and the Terracotta Army near Xi'an. The country is now developing new attractions to pull in more tourists, particularly in the field of sports. In 2004, a huge, new, world-championship racing track was opened as part of the Formula One circuit. And amidst much controversy, because of its human rights record, Beijing hosted the 2008 Olympic Games.

The phenomenal growth of cities such as Shanghai has become a tourist attraction in itself. Boat trips are taken to view its ultra-modern skyline that includes the futuristic Oriental Pearl TV Tower – one of the tallest buildings in the world. In contrast, other tourists are attracted to China by the remoteness of some of the areas in the west, such as Tibet.

Although overseas travel for Chinese people is still restricted by the government, some of these restrictions are being lifted. In 1993 just under 4 million Chinese people travelled abroad; by 2006 this number was 34.5 million. In 2004, an agreement was reached between China and the European Union which makes it easier for Chinese citizens to apply for tourist visas to 29 European nations that have been granted 'approved destination status' by China.

Focus on: The Beijing Olympics, 2008

The decision to award the 2008 Olympic Games to Beijing was highly controversial. Human rights organizations such as Human Rights Watch and Amnesty International expressed concern that by granting the Olympic Games to Beijing, the world was condoning China's human rights record. Some Chinese dissidents claimed that China would use the Olympic Games to present itself as a global power with an acceptable human rights record. When thousands of international sports people and journalists arrived in China for the Games, there was intense media coverage. Some believe that placing China under the world's spotlight will have encouraged improvements in human rights. Others believe China's control and suppression of the media is too strong for there to be lasting change.

▶ This clock in Tiananmen Square, Beijing, was used to count down to the 2008 Olympic Games.

CHAPTER 13

Environment and Conservation

China's environment is paying the price for the country's rapid economic development. There are several factors that are having a major effect on the environment: the pressures of supporting such a large population with the produce from the relatively small area of land that is suitable for cultivation, extremes of temperature and rainfall, and the phenomenally rapid rate of industrialization.

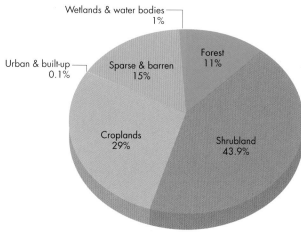

▲ Types of habitat

▲ This picture of a snow leopard was taken on a wildlife reserve in northern China. It is estimated that there are around 2,000 snow leopards in China, but they are seriously threatened by poaching, habitat loss and shortage of prey.

WILDLIFE UNDER THREAT

The diversity of wildlife in China is among the greatest in the world, with a huge variety of both plant and animal species. However, many animals in China are on the endangered species list including, most famously, the giant panda, the snow leopard, tigers, ibis and elephants. These animals are threatened with extinction by a combination of loss of habitat to human development, illegal hunting and natural disasters such as floods.

DAMS

Many animal conservationists are worried about the number of hydroelectric power projects being planned in China. The construction of a

Did you know?

By 2010 China plans to increase the number of its nature reserves to 1,800. They will cover about 16.14 per cent of the country's territory.

dam seriously decreases the flow of water downstream from the dam, and has a major impact on river habitats. There is particular concern for the *baiji*, a type of freshwater dolphin that lives in the Yangtze River. In 2006 the *baiji* was thought to be extinct, although one dolphin was spotted a year later. The construction of the Three Gorges Dam has significantly changed the *baiji*'s habitat, and the *baiji* is expected to become extinct in the near future. In 2004 plans for a huge dam system on the Nu River in southern China were shelved for environmental reasons, but many other dams are planned elsewhere.

Environmental and conservation data

- Forested area as percentage of total land area: 11
- Protected area as percentage of total land area: 11
- Number of protected areas: 822

SPECIES DIVERSITY

Category	Known species (1992-02)	Threatened species (2002)
Mammals	394	79
Breeding birds	618	74
Reptiles	424	31
Amphibians	340	1
Fish	395	32
Plants	32,200	168

Source: World Resources Institute

Focus on: The giant panda

The giant panda is one of the best-known symbols of China. It is found only in southwest China and lives exclusively on a diet of bamboo shoots. It is one of the world's most endangered species and faces threats from the loss of its habitat, and from poaching. The Chinese government has set up more than thirty reserves to protect the giant panda, and near Chengdu in Sichuan Province there is an important breeding centre. Some of the pandas at this centre are raised in such a way that they can be reintroduced to the wild. It is estimated that there are only about 1,600 giant pandas remaining in the world.

▶ A giant panda eats bamboo shoots in Chengdu, Sichuan Province.

▲ A girl covers her nose and mouth to keep out dust in the centre of Congjiang, Guizhou Province, southeast China.

DEFORESTATION

Over the last fifty years, vast areas of China's forests have been cut down for construction purposes and for fuel. This deforestation has caused soil erosion, particularly in areas of high rainfall, and has had a devastating impact on river catchments, increasing the incidence of flooding in some of China's major river regions. In 1998, devastating floods along the Yangtze that killed 4,000 people were partly blamed on excessive deforestation along the upper reaches of the Yangtze and other rivers. As a result, China implemented a complete ban on logging. However, the demand for timber remained the same, so Chinese imports of timber rocketed. The increase in the amount of timber exported from Russia and Southeast Asia has put huge pressure on forests in these regions.

DESERTIFICATION

Desertification is a major problem in China, affecting nearly a quarter of the country's total land area. The biggest problems are in the northwest, where the deserts are growing at an alarming rate. One reason for the increase in desertification lies in the rapid expansion of cities in the east of the country, reducing the amount of farmland available and leading to the opening up of new areas in the northwest to agriculture. Land has been cleared of trees and ploughed up for crops, exposing the thin soil to erosion from wind and rain. In other places overgrazing has meant that animals have stripped the land of its vegetation. In the Takla Makan Desert, sand frequently buries houses and crops. However, the effects of desertification are felt far beyond the deserts of the northwest, and sandstorms often darken the skies over China's eastern cities, thousands of kilometres away from the desert (see page 17). Measures to fight desertification include projects to plant trees, but the prospect of a

Chinese 'dustbowl' and its impacts on food production have serious implications for China's ability to produce the large amounts of food it needs to feed its vast population.

POLLUTION

China has developed its industries with little thought for the environment. Its high consumption of coal has made the country the world's second largest producer of carbon emissions after the United States. Many Chinese cities are often shrouded in a thick smog of pollution, with unhealthy levels of toxic particles in the air. Many rivers in China are also polluted by chemicals, untreated waste from factories and untreated sewage.

China is now engaged in a massive effort to clean up its own environment and consequently the environment of the world. Since 1966, China has shut down 60,000 inefficient industrial boilers, while hundreds of small power stations have also been closed. In 1993 the government introduced laws abolishing ozone-depleting substances. Since then it has funded the exploration of alternative, more environmentally friendly technology as well as energy sources such as wind power and solar energy.

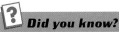

Did you know?

According to the World Health Organization, some of the world's most polluted cities are in China. They include Linfen, Yangquan and Datong, all in coal-producing Shanxi Province. Beijing, which introduced measures to improve its air quality for the 2008 Olympic Games, was number 28 on the list.

▼ Factories belch out smoke and fumes at an industrial complex on the outskirts of Beijing.

CHAPTER 14

Future Challenges

China's headlong dash for growth has raised many concerns: about the environment, the size of the population, the often appalling working conditions, the effects on traditional Chinese life and culture and the increasing gap between the rich and the poor.

PUBLIC WELFARE

The cost of supporting such a huge population places a burden on the state for resources such as education and health, both of which are vital to ensure the country's economic development. Like many other countries, China needs to face up to the challenge of the spread of the HIV/AIDS virus.

Eventually, China will have to pay the costs of its One-Child Policy. From around 2020 there will be a reduction in the labour force and the population will begin to age. As the country's economy continues to grow and to transform the whole country at an unprecedented rate, pressure to relax the One-Child Policy is likely to intensify. The imbalance between young men and women poses a major threat to the healthy,

▼ The stunning interior of Pudong International Airport in Shanghai which opened in 1999. Shanghai now has two international airports, reflecting its status as one of the main hubs of China's economic development.

harmonious and sustainable growth of the nation's population. Making women more equal to men in terms of pay, and therefore in their ability to support their families, may prevent families from wanting only boy babies.

ECONOMIC CHANGES

The sustainability of China's economic boom is in question. Some experts think that economic growth has been too fast and unplanned. The changes in the economy have failed to benefit the majority of the Chinese population, and the people who are employed in factories, fuelling China's economic growth, often work in sweatshop conditions. The initial advantages China has had will not last if employment costs rise. If this were to happen, foreign investors may choose to relocate to other countries where labour costs are lower, such as India.

In response to some of these problems, the Chinese goverment is considering measures to control the pace of economic growth through restraints on investment and lending. By slowing the pace of growth, the government would hope to curb inflation that, if left uncontrolled, would drive up labour costs and reduce China's global competitiveness. There is already evidence that China's booming economy and incredible demand for commodities (in 2008 China consumed almost a third of the world's steel) is driving up world prices. Preventing the economy from 'overheating' is a key challenge for the Chinese government.

CHINA'S UNIQUE CULTURE

More links with other countries through economic development and the growth of the tourist industry mean that China is increasingly coming into contact with Western ideas. Many people welcome these new influences, but others worry that traditional Chinese culture may suffer. China has a difficult balancing act to perform in the future as it struggles to preserve its unique culture while at the same time emerging as a new world superpower.

? Did you know?

In October 2003 China sent its first astronaut, Yang Liwei, into space. The flight made China only the third country in the world to launch a manned spacecraft into orbit (after the United States and Russia). This event was seen as a symbol of the huge progress China has made and its ambitions for the future.

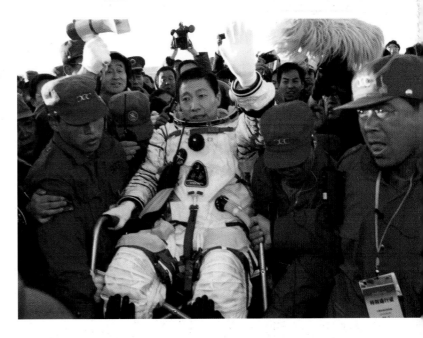

▲ China's first astronaut, Yang Liwei, waves to a large crowd after his safe return to earth on 16 October 2003.

Timeline

c.2070-c.1600 BC China's first dynasty, the Xia.

c.1046-c.221 BC Chou (Zhou) dynasty

771-481 BC Chou dynasty.

c.551-c.479 BC Life of philosopher Confucius (K'ung Fu-tzu).

221-206 BC China is unified under the Qin dynasty.

206 BC-AD 220 Flourishing of intellectual and artistic life under the Han dynasty.

220-280 Wei, Shu and Wu: a period of chaos and decline as China is divided into three kingdoms.

265-589 Jin, Sixteen Kingdoms and Northern and Southern Dynasties.

581-618 Reunification and centralization of government under the Sui dynasty.

618-907 High point in Chinese civilization under the T'ang dynasty.

907-60 Five dynasties: China breaks up into separate states.

960-1279 Reunification of China under the Song dynasty.

1215 Genghis Khan captures Beijing.

1271-95 Marco Polo's journey to China.

1279-1368 Mongol Yuan dynasty.

1368-1644 Ming dynasty.

1644-1911 Ch'ing or Manchu dynasty.

1839–42 First Opium War.

1856-1860 Second Opium War.

1894-5 War with Japan.

1911 Last emperor is deposed.

1912 Sun Yat-Sen declares China a republic.

1919 Fourth of May movement in Beijing.

1921 Chinese Communist Party founded.

1931 Japan invades Manchuria.

1934-5 Mao Zedong leads the 'Long March'.

1937-45 Sino-Japanese War.

1949 Chinese Communists defeat the Nationalists and Mao Zedong proclaims the People's Republic of China.

1958 The Great Leap Forward begins.

1966 Mao Zedong launches the Great Proletarian Cultural Revolution.

1972 US President Richard Nixon visits China.

1976 Death of Mao Zedong.

1978 Start of economic modernization led by Deng Xiaoping.

1979 Start of One-Child Policy.

1989 Government troops put down Tiananmen Square demonstration.

1993 Work starts on Three Gorges Dam on the Yangtze River.

1997 Hong Kong reverts to China.

1999 Chinese government bans Falun Gong movement.

2001 China joins the World Trade Organization.

2002 Work starts on the South-to-North Water Transfer Project.

2002-3 Global outbreak of SARS begins in China.

2003 China sends its first astronaut, Yang Liwei, into space.

2008 Beijing hosts the 29th Olympic Games.

Glossary

Acupuncture A centuries-old method of maintaining and restoring harmony in the body by piercing certain points with thin needles.

Alluvial Describes clay and silt that are carried by fast-moving streams and rivers and then deposited when the waters slow down. Alluvial soils are usually very fertile.

Atheist Describes those who do not believe in a god or gods.

Autonomous Self-governing. In China, the five autonomous regions (*zizhiqu*) have some self-government but remain under the control of the central Communist government.

Bourgeois A member of the middle, or in Communist countries capitalist, class.

Cede To surrender or give up.

Collective farms In Communist countries, a group of farms owned by the state and run by the community.

Communism A political system that abolishes private ownership and emphasizes common ownership of property and the means of production.

Democracy A political system in which representatives are chosen by the people in free elections.

Desertification The process by which fertile land is degraded into barren desert.

Detention Custody or confinement.

Dissident Someone who speaks out against the policies of their government.

Dustbowl An arid region in which wind erosion causes dust storms.

Dynasty A series of rulers from the same family who succeed one another in power.

Elitist The belief that a particular group of people is superior to other groups.

Ethnic Classification of humans according to racial origins.

Floodplain An area of open land through which a river flows and which is sometimes covered by its flood waters.

Free market An economic system that is largely controlled by the laws of supply and demand rather than by government regulations.

Freight Commercial goods carried by lorries, ships, trains and aeroplanes.

Guerrilla A member of an irregular armed force.

Hydroelectric power The production of electricity by harnessing the power of moving water.

Industrialization The process of developing factories and manufacturing on a large scale.

Inflation The measure of the increase in the general level of prices in a country.

Infrastructure The basic facilities and equipment needed for a country to function.

Martial arts Various styles of armed and unarmed combat developed in the East and usually practised today as a sport.

Nationalism A strong commitment to the independence, culture and interests of one's own country.

Nomadic Describes people who move from place to place rather than living in a settlement.

Opium A drug produced from the juice of the opium poppy which can be addictive if misused.

Plateau An area of high, level land.

Species A group of plants or animals that share common features.

Tariff A tax on imports.

Topography The shape of the surface features of the earth.

Totalitarian Describes a form of government that is highly centralized, which controls all aspects of life in a country, and which suppresses opposition.

Typhoon A violent, rotating storm in the West Pacific or Indian oceans, also known as a cyclone.

Urbanization The movement of people from rural areas to towns and cities.

Further Information

BOOKS TO READ

River Journey: Yangtze
Rob Bowden
(Wayland, 2005)

Continents: Asia
Rob Bowden
(Wayland, 2007)

Cambridge Illustrated History: China
Patricia Buckley Ebrey
(CUP, 1999)

Eyewitness Guides: China
Arthur Cotterell
(Dorling Kindersley, 1994)

Countries of the World: China
Carole Goddard
(Evans Publishing, 2007)

The Changing Face of China
Stephen Keeler
(Wayland, 2007)

Modern China: An Illustrated History
J.A.G. Roberts
(Sutton Publishing, 2000)

NOVELS

Wild Swans: Three Daughters of China
Jung Chang
(Harper Perennial, 2004)

USEFUL WEBSITES

www.chinadaily.com.cn
China's English-language newspaper online.

http://www.economist.com/countries/China/
Information about China and its economy.

http://www.china.org.cn
General information about China.

http://www.cia.gov/library/publications/the-world-factbook/geos/ch.html
The CIA World Factbook gives up-to-date facts and figures for China.

Index

About the Authors

Ali Brownlie Bojang is a former teacher of humanities and an education officer for Oxfam. She has written a number of books for young people as well as course materials for teachers.

Nicola Barber is the author of many non-fiction children's books, specialising in geography, history and the arts.